Traditional
Houses
from
Around the World

A. G. Smith

DOVER PUBLICATIONS, INC.
Mineola, New York

Copyright

Copyright © 2000 by A. G. Smith
All rights reserved under Pan American and International Copyright Conventions.

Bibliographical Note

Traditional Houses from Around the World is a new work, first published by Dover Publications, Inc., in 2000.

DOVER *Pictorial Archive* SERIES

This book belongs to the Dover Pictorial Archive Series. You may use the designs and illustrations for graphics and crafts applications, free and without special permission, provided that you include no more than four in the same publication or project. (For permission for additional use, please write to Permissions Department, Dover Publications, Inc., 31 East 2nd Street, Mineola, N.Y. 11501.)

However, republication or reproduction of any illustration by any other graphic service, whether it be in a book or in any other design resource, is strictly prohibited.

International Standard Book Number: 0-486-41322-5

Manufactured in the United States of America
Dover Publications, Inc., 31 East 2nd Street, Mineola, N.Y. 11501

Publisher's Note

The universal need for shelter is the subject of this informative coloring book, for which artist A. G. Smith has created 45 remarkably detailed renderings of traditional housing around the world. Represented on these pages are dwellings from Africa, Asia, Australia, Europe, and North and South America.

Some will be familiar—the Swiss chalet, the pioneer log cabin, the Inuit igloo, and the Plains Indian tepee. Less familiar, perhaps, are the Dogon cliff dwellings or Indonesian Batak house. All of the builders have followed tradition in maintaining housing that suits their environment or reflects treasured cultural values. The Dogon cliff dwellers in Mali, for example, may group eight buildings together because that number shows respect for the eight chief Dogon ancestors. Some building methods have persisted for thousands of years, such as the reed houses built by Marsh Arabs in Iraq. These structures, resembling those built 7,000 years ago, make use of the native materials of reed and papyrus. The Marsh Arabs continue to build these shelters even though they are flammable and subject to insect infestation.

Traditional dwellings utilize natural materials from the environment, such as wood, bamboo and grass reeds, stone, and adobe, that are found around the world—bamboo and reeds in parts of Africa, as well as South America and Bali; animal skins in Plains Indian tepees in North America, Bedouin tents in Arabia, and Lapp mountain tents in northern Europe; adobe in Pueblo Indian, African, and southern European dwellings.

Enjoy coloring these finely detailed renderings of traditional housing as you learn about many of the world's intriguing cultures, who have both adapted to, and made good use of, their surroundings. Houses are arranged alphabetically by the continent on which they appear, and then alphabetically by country, state, or region within each continent.

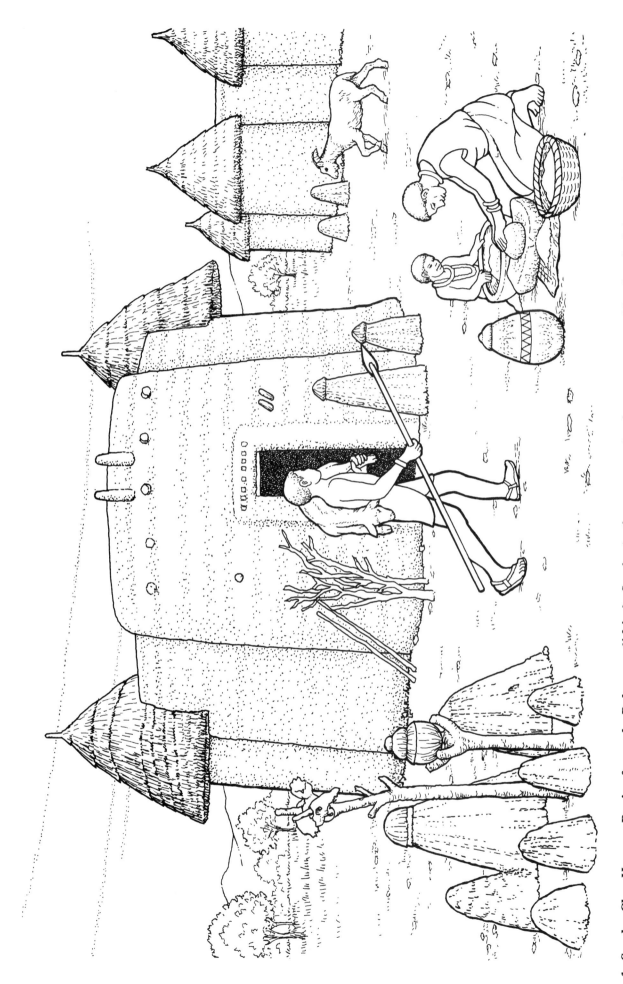

1. Somba Clay Houses, Benin, formerly Dahomey (Africa). Somba is the name, retained from colonial times, given to the people living on a plateau west of the Atacora mountain chain in northern Benin, West Africa. The dwellings of the Somba are windowless structures possessing two- or three-story circular towers topped by thatched (covered by straw or reed) turrets. The Somba houses resemble small castles. The roofs serve as a lookout for approaching visitors; there may be sleeping huts on the roof as well.

2. Masai House, Kenya (Africa). The Masai are nomadic cattle herders who live in East Africa. Their low, loaf-shaped dwellings—*manyatta*—are made of a wooden frame covered with leaves, mud, and cow dung. The Masai women are the house builders, spending perhaps a month on each structure. The manyatta are arranged in a circle in order to enclose the Masai's cattle. The manyatta may be protected by a plastic sheet during the rainy season. These windowless structures generally are used for sleeping or for shelter from the rain.

3. Dogon Cliff Dwellings, Mali (Africa). The Dogon live south of the Sahara Desert, where they make their home among cliffs that reach up to 1,000 feet. In this isolated, harsh land, the Dogon have built tiny houses of adobe, a material ideally suited to the dry, sun-drenched climate. The houses' thick clay walls help keep the heat out. Grain is stored in straw-topped rectangular buildings next to the dwellings. The main room is both the sleeping quarters and the woman's workroom, where she spins and weaves.

4. Moroccan Brick Houses, Morocco (North Africa).
This town house is a vertical structure designed to offer a solution to the overcrowding found in cities by stacking rooms and maximizing the use of the limited urban space. The tall town houses shown here provide shade from the intense North African sun for passersby in the urban alleyways. The flat roofs of these brick buildings can be used by families for relaxing, or for sleeping on a cool night. The thick walls keep out the heat. Small windows, few in number, help keep the interior of the town house cool.

5. Painted Mud House, Nigeria (Africa). The mud houses of the Hausa people are built with rich red clay, baked by the African sun. The distinctive exteriors of these dwellings are painted with intricate designs in vivid colors. In addition to the painted decorations, the builders add sculptural designs, creating a vibrant appearance for these mud dwellings. The influence of Islam on the Hausa can be seen in the complex Islamic designs that adorn these homes.

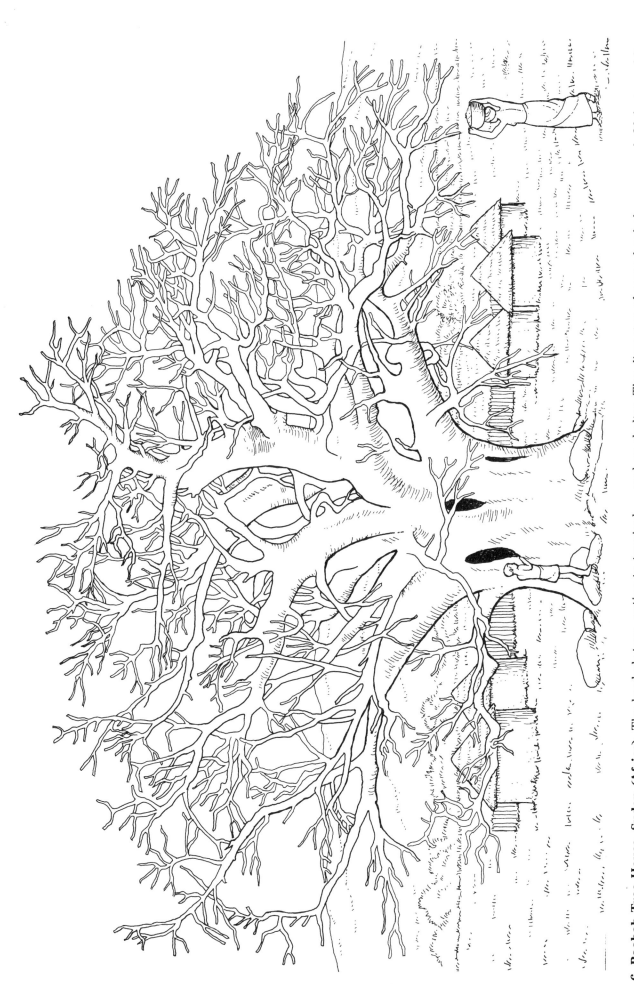

6. Baobab Tree House, Sudan (Africa). The baobab tree, native to tropical Africa, offers tempting possibilities as a dwelling place because of its massive size. Africans such as the Sudanese discovered that they could hollow out the moist, spongy interior of the baobab's trunk and use it both as a hiding place and as shelter. The diameter of some baobabs can reach 30 feet, enabling a family to live inside the trunk comfortably. Africans also use the hollowed-out space to store water.

7. Bedouin Tent, Arabia (Asia). The Bedouin tent is commonly associated with the Arabian deserts. The nomadic Bedouin way of life has been exposed to modern influences, but Bedouin still create their tents from animal skins, usually camel. As many as forty of these skins might be used to make a tent. A movable strip is often added to the tent to catch passing breezes or to protect the inhabitants from sandstorms. There are separate areas for the men and the women. The tent suits the nomadic existence, being easy to put up and quick to take down.

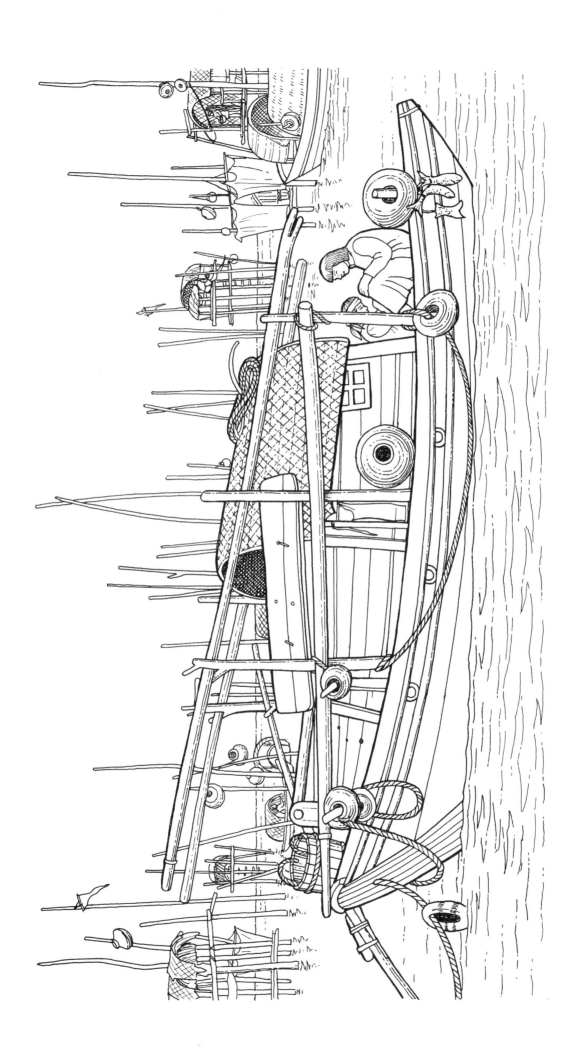

8. Houseboat, South China (Asia). Millions of people make their homes permanently on houseboats, especially in Southeast Asia. The advantage of this type of living arrangement is the proximity to the water for fishing, washing, and traveling in an area geared to houseboat living. Shopping can be done at nearby commercial boats, and varied services catering to the houseboat dwellers are available as well. Not all who live in houseboats do so by choice; many are refugees, forced from the land, who have no other place to live.

9. Tree House, India (Asia). The tree house shown here serves as an excellent lookout for spotting approaching visitors, friendly and unfriendly alike. It rises over the permanent house below, solidly constructed of wood and thatch, at the base of the tree.

The open-sided wood-and-thatch tree house rests upon the branches of a tall tree such as the peepul, which grows up to 100 feet tall. The tree house can be used as a temporary shelter, but is generally impractical as a permanent dwelling.

10. Batak House, Indonesia (Asia). The Bataks live in the northern and central highlands on the island of Sumatra. Because Sumatra has no dry season, housing is raised off the damp ground by wooden platforms. Enormous sloping roofs of wooden shingles or thatch cap the handful of houses built in a closely knit Batak village. The villagers climb a ladder to enter their houses. The water buffalo is sacred to the Bataks, and carvings suggesting buffalo horns decorate the houses (seen here at the front corners). The fine craftsmanship of the Batak builders includes intricate geometric designs carved into the house's upper wall.

11. Turkoman Yurt, Iran (Asia). The Turkoman people travel the Iranian desert in search of water and grazing land for their animals. The women pitch tents, called *yurts*, setting up a wooden framework and then covering it with felt that they have made from sheep's wool. They may use several layers of this waterproof felt during winter. The yurts have separate men's and women's areas. The Turkoman carry their lightweight tents with them as they wander. Stovepipes have replaced chimneys as modernization has touched this traditional lifestyle. The yurt is also used by other Central Asian peoples.

12. Marsh Arab Reed House, Iraq (Asia). The Marsh Arabs live in the delta of the Tigris and Euphrates rivers. This traditional style of building has existed for 7,000 years. Using reeds that grow to over 20 feet high and papyrus 10 feet wide, the Marsh Arabs build their houses on man-made islands. Bundles of reeds are planted in the earth in columns; the tops are bent and tied to make an arch. More bundles fill in between the columns, until a "tunnel" is created. Wall mats can be rolled up to let in breezes.

13. Kibbutz House, Israel (Asia). An Israeli kibbutz is a community whose members work together and share in the land and property. Typical kibbutz products are citrus fruits, grains, and cotton. Many *kibbutzim* (plural) have a separate children's house, where the cooperative's children live apart from their parents; however, some children may go home to sleep. There are farm buildings and a school and, perhaps, a community store, where members get clothing or other necessary items in exchange for their work on the kibbutz. Kibbutzim eat together in a communal dining room.

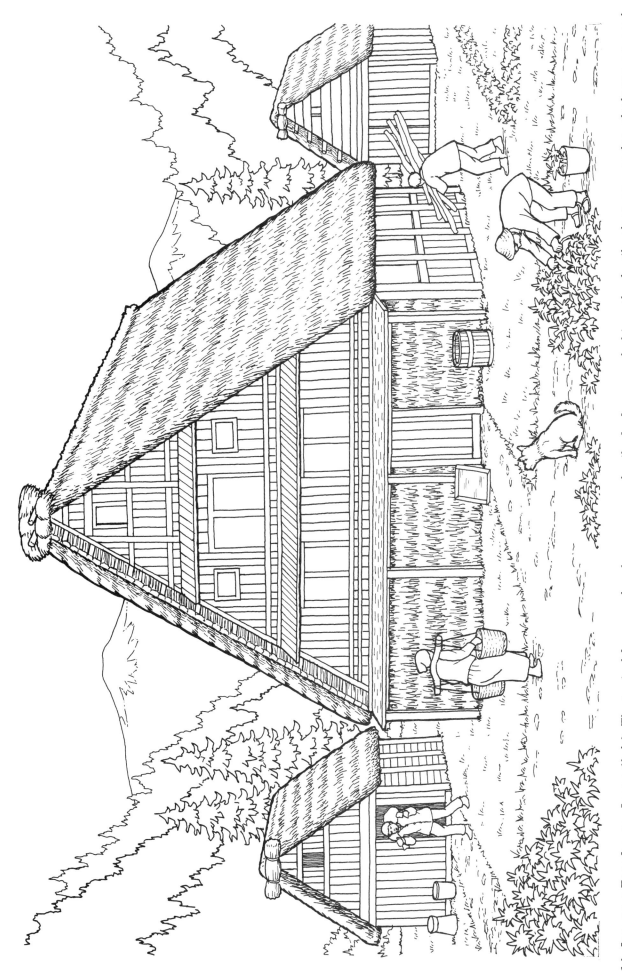

14. Japanese Farmhouse, Japan (Asia). The typical Japanese farmhouse was built of wood, had a roof thatched with reeds, and window screens made of straw. It was common for the farm animals to sleep under the roof with the family. In Japanese fashion, the family slept on wooden platforms covered with straw mats. Fire safety was (and still is) a natural concern for the occupants of a structure made of such flammable materials.

15. Water House, Thailand (Asia). As can be seen in the picture above, the water houses of Thailand are a solution to the quest for living space in a watery environment. Houses built on stilts keep the inhabitants safe from flooding, while enabling them to navigate the water for trade. Forked logs pro-vide support for the wooden structure, which is topped by a sloping thatched roof. The houses are built with fenced-in balconies from which the inhabi-tants can observe the activity on the water.

16. Mountain House, Tibet (Asia). Tibetan houses traditionally were constructed of stone or sun-dried brick walls. Shingles made from pine trees were positioned on the roof and then held down with stones. There were few windows in these structures because of the gale winds that blow in this mountainous region. An opening in the roof let out smoke from cooking and heating. Wooden ladders were used to move from one building level to another. The house to the rear displays Tibetan prayer flags, hung to bring good luck to the villagers.

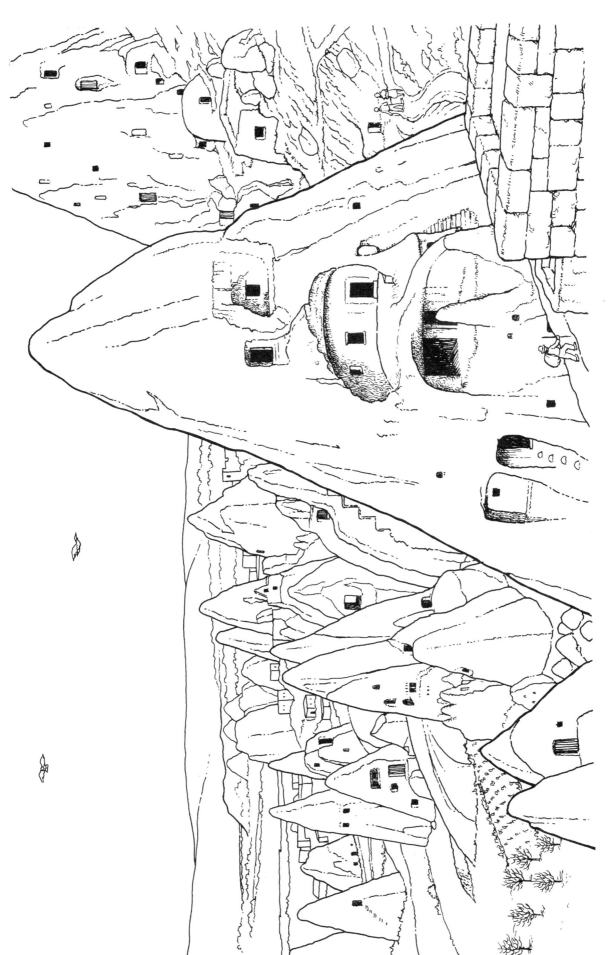

17. Cave Houses, Turkey (Asia). For over two thousand years, inhabitants of the Cappadocia region have taken advantage of its soft volcanic rock to carve out houses, churches, and monasteries. The builders provide wooden windows and doors, place carpets on the dirt floors, and paint the cave's walls. They even carve out staircases, leading to upstairs rooms, from the malleable rock. These multi-storied structures have been continually adapted for human living over the years.

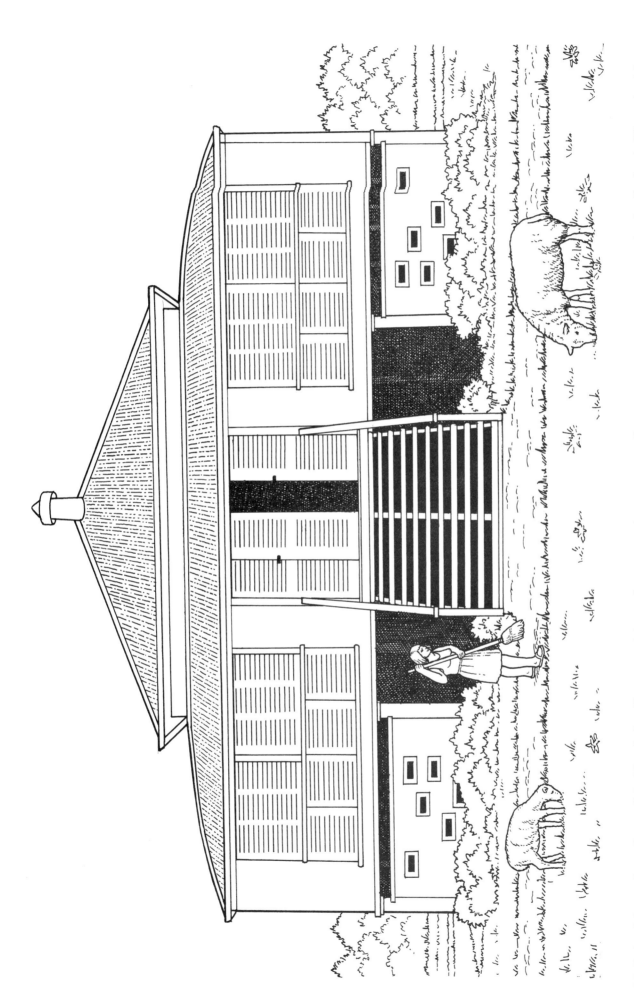

18. Raised Bungalow (Australia). The "inland" region of Australia—west of the Dividing Ranges and of the continent's chief cities of Sydney, Melbourne, Brisbane, and Adelaide—contains the flat land that serves as pasture for part of the continent's sheep-raising industry. "Sheep stations" of a hundred square miles or more are not uncommon in the Outback. The raised bungalow shown here contains large shutters which can be closed to keep out the midday heat prevalent in the Outback, and opened to let in evening breezes.

19. Aboriginal Bark Hut (Australia). This shelter of easily available natural material reveals the simplicity of living arrangements for these original inhabitants of the Australian continent. Aborigines for generations have constructed dwellings from large sheets of tree bark, which they drape over a post-and-lintel arrangement of sturdy branches. This temporary shelter has suited the Aborigines, as they roam great distances looking for food. After the arrival of British settlers in Australia, changes took place in Aboriginal life, and the traditional way of life has changed.

20. Farmhouse, Denmark (Europe). When people began to plant crops and to farm in one location, they constructed permanent dwellings. Ancient farmhouses were made of logs in wooded areas, or of bricks or stone. European farmhouses originally were simple buildings consisting of one floor, perhaps one room. The farmhouse was shelter for the farm family; additional housing existed for hired workers. Animals were often housed with the farm family. A central fireplace vented cooking and heating fumes through a hole in the roof. Wood and thatch (a roof covering made of straw or reeds) were used to build a rectangular house with a slanted roof.

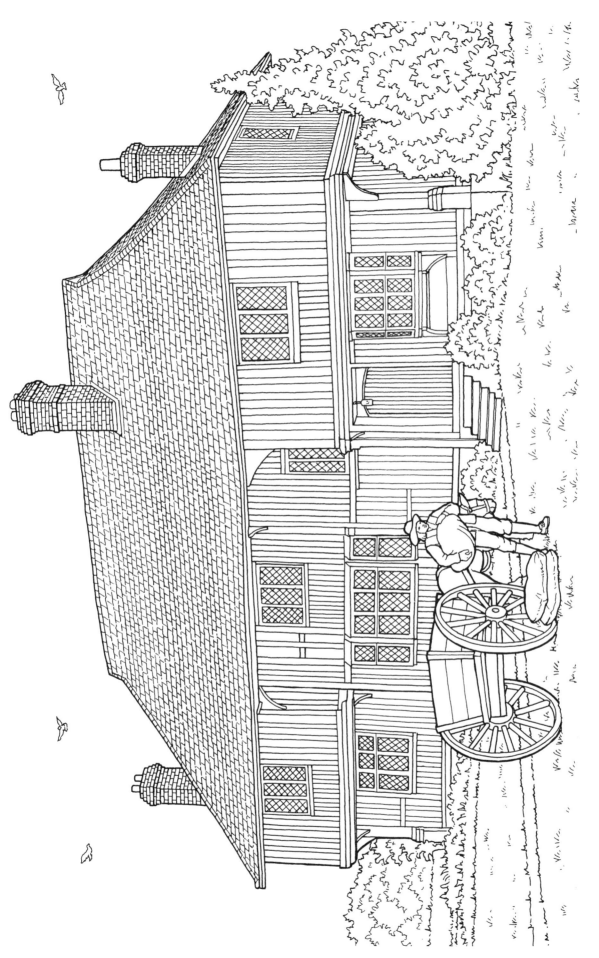

21. Half-Timbered House, England (Europe). Half-timbering consists of wood beams arranged vertically, and the spaces filled in with mud-plastered twigs (known as "wattle and daub" construction). This type of architecture became common in the late 15th to late 16th centuries. Centuries-old half-timbered houses can be found in the English countryside, but they have not been built in London since 1666, the year of the great London fire. A fire hazard, half-timbered construction in the capital city was banned after that time.

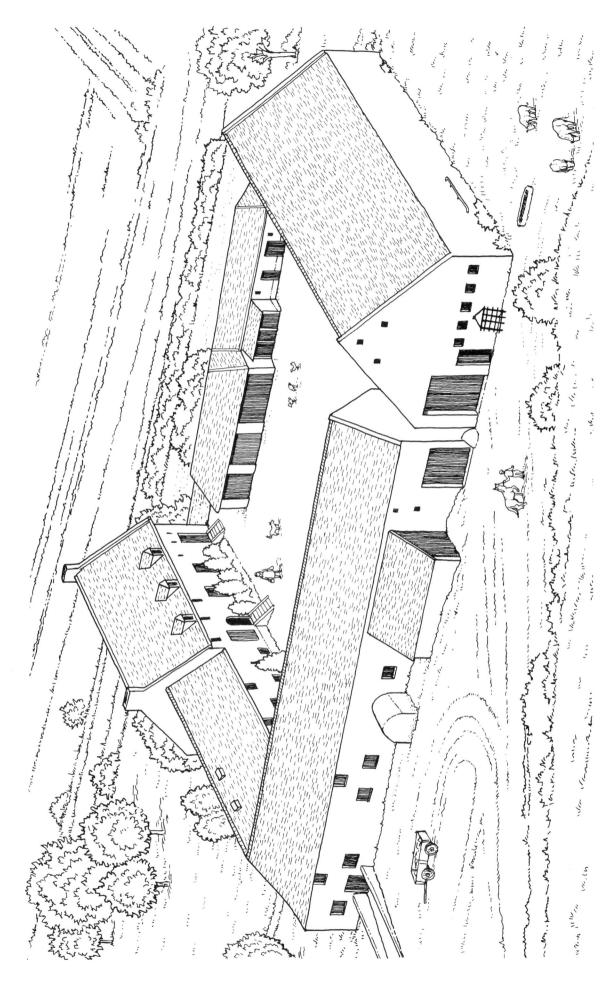

22. Farmhouse, France (Europe). Traditionally, a French farm was owned and operated by a single family and was quite small. In fact, until recently, half of all French farms consisted of fewer than 30 acres. However, large manor houses, such as the one shown here in northern France, hired paid workers. This manor house has an enclosed courtyard, creating a fortress-like appear-ance. There is housing for the farm's owners as well as their hired workers; in addition, there is storage space for livestock and crops. Farmhouses such as this—some hundreds of years old—can still be encountered in the French countryside.

23. Town House, Northern Germany (Europe). Town houses were built up vertically, rather than spread out horizontally, in order to maximize the use of space in towns, where real estate was at a premium. The house shown here exemplifies the use of half-timbered construction; wooden beams were arranged vertically and filled in with brick. This town house has a gabled roof—the two slopes of the roof form a triangle. Glass-paned windows permitted some light to enter this solid structure. This northern European building style flourished between 1400 and 1600.

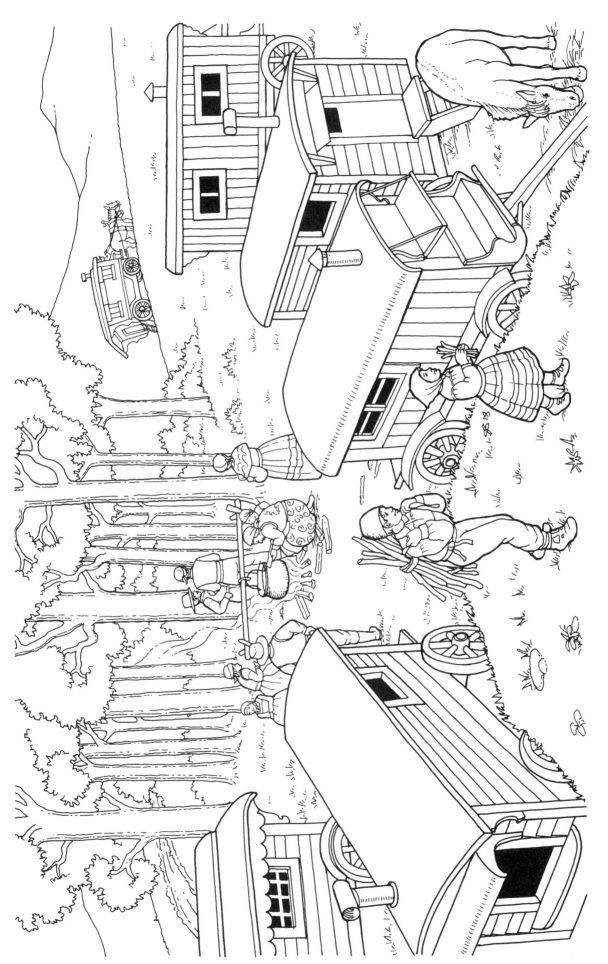

24. Gypsy Wagon, Great Britain and Central Europe (Europe). The gypsies of Europe, Great Britain, and Ireland have lived in structures ranging from caves and mud huts to tents and cottages. The gypsy wagon is popularly associated with these wandering people who originally came from India. The wagon, whether horse-drawn or motorized, contains a sleeping area and wooden furniture. Some caravans, or *vardoes*, as they were known in Romany, were known in Romany, as they were known in Romany, contained a wood-burning stove. Furniture was decorated with traditional patterns.

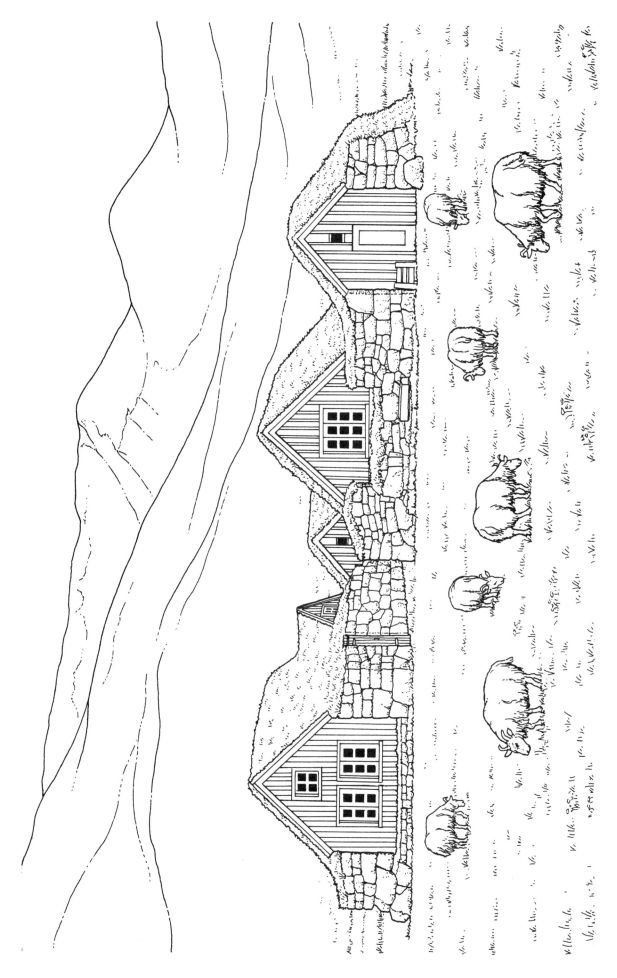

25. Farmhouse, Iceland (Europe). Iceland combines rugged mountain ranges with numerous active volcanoes. Its economy relies heavily on fishing, but until 1930, about a third of the country's population was involved in farming. That percentage has dropped to the single digits in recent years. Livestock raising and dairy farming occupy the farmers who have clung to this way of life. The Icelandic farms shown above combine wood with stone and sod roofing. The fallen snow resting on the sod roof acted as insulation for the farmhouse during the winter months.

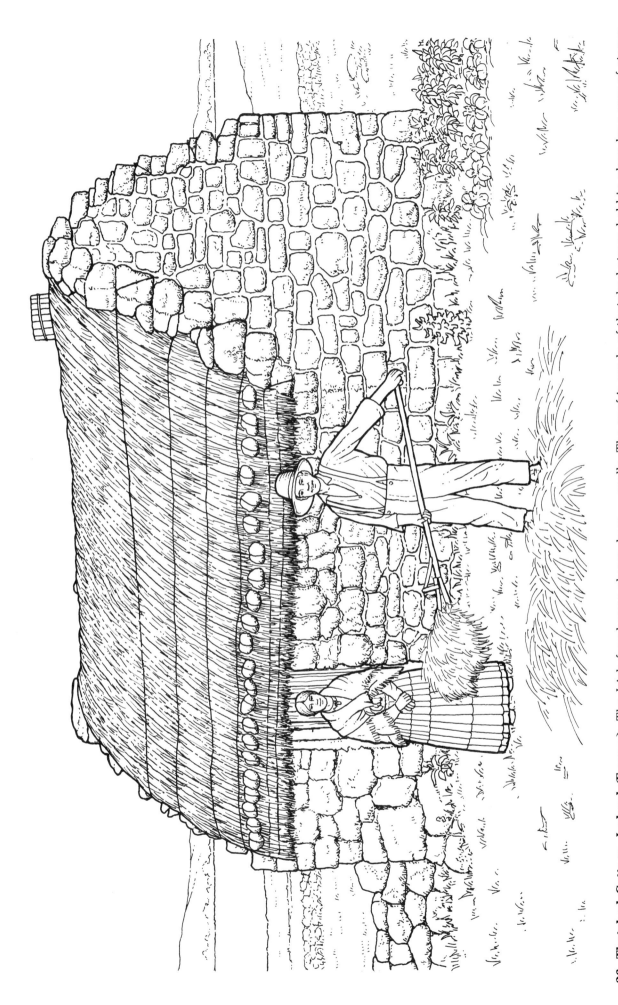

26. Thatched Cottage, Ireland (Europe). The Irish farmhouse shown here was built using numerous irregularly shaped rocks to produce a rough-hewn type of housing for the farm family. Mortar (a binding material usually made of water, sand, and lime) has been used to hold together the stones in the walls. The roof is made of thatched straw, held in place by a row of stones. Traditionally, those living in the countryside took advantage of the abundant peat (a substance formed by decomposed plants) for their fuel needs.

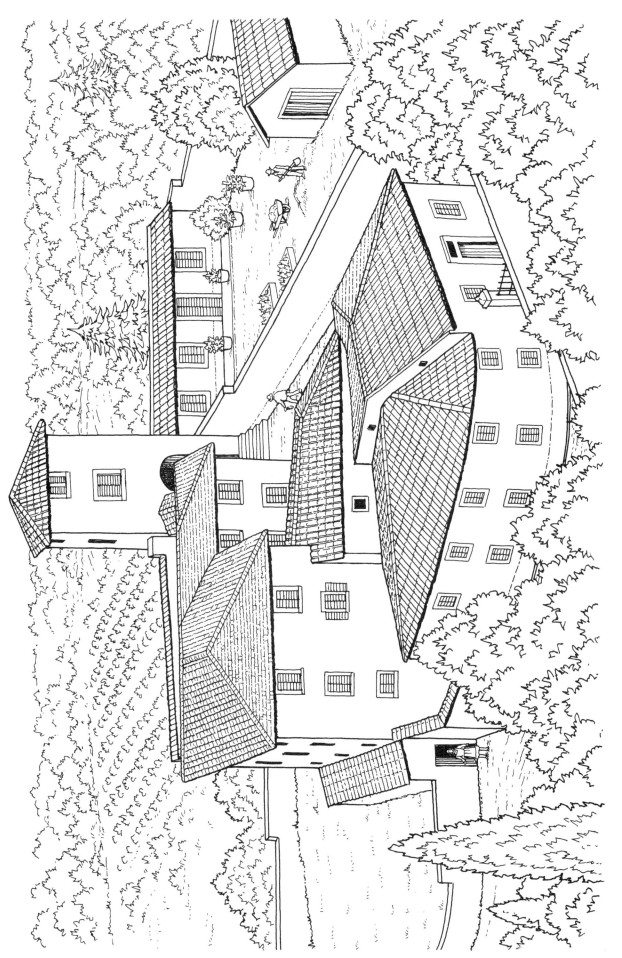

27. House with courtyard, Italy (Europe). The construction of this country home denotes privacy, as can be seen in the high wall enclosing the property. This sprawling collection of buildings contains many shuttered windows, closed during the warm weather. Part of the compound probably contained living quarters for the servants and farmhands. Here is an interesting mix of multi-storied structures, ranging from the single level next to the tower, to the two- and four-storied wings, and culminating in the tower itself. The sloping roofs are covered in tile, the material preferred by the ancient Romans.

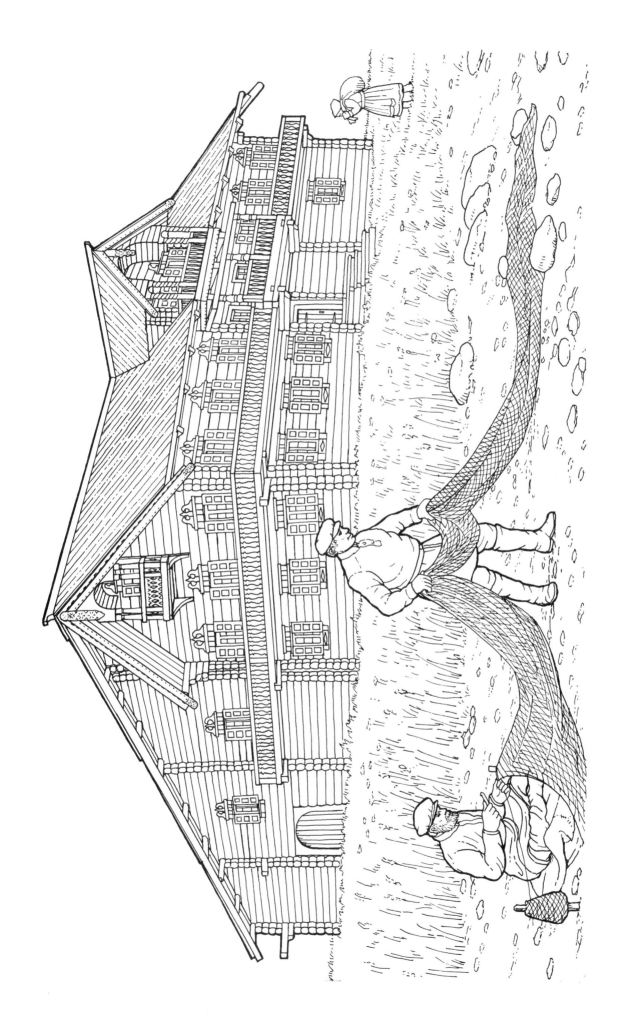

28. Farmhouse, Karelia, Russian Federation (Europe). Karelia has changed hands among Sweden, Finland, and Russia (the former Soviet Union) numerous times since the 12th century. Today, it is part of the Russian Federation, although its people are racially identified with the Finns. This typical northern European timber construction has logs laid crosswise at the corners; wooden planks are used for the roof as well. Some of the exterior woodwork is carved in traditional motifs. The second-story balconies and a third-story dormer provide lookouts and places to relax.

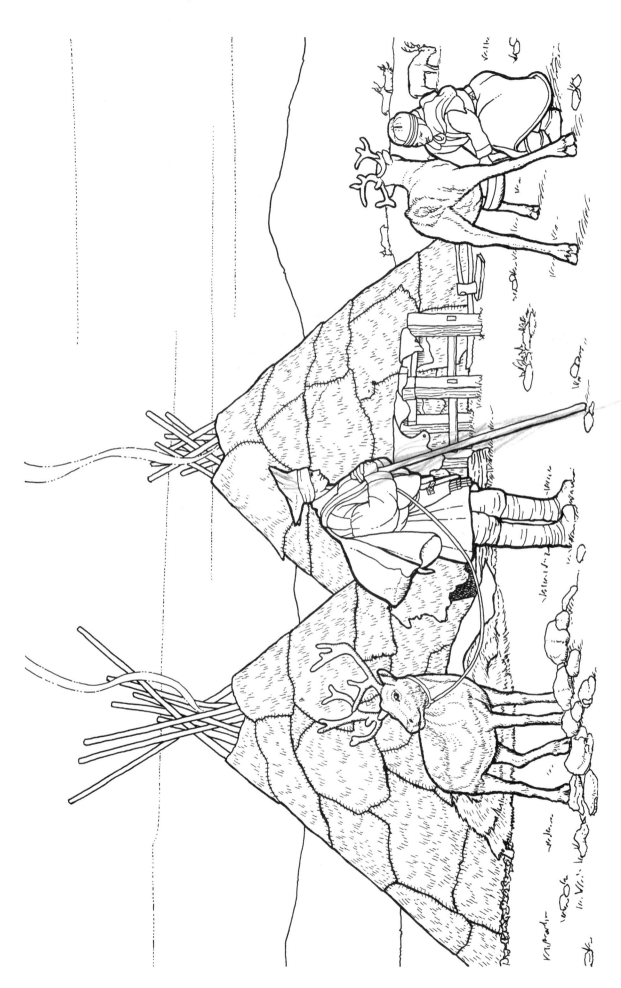

29. Lapp Mountain Tent, Lapland (Europe). The Lapp people, known as Samis, live above the Arctic Circle near Norway, Sweden, Finland, and Russia. The Samis are reindeer herders whose need for shelter traditionally has been satisfied by a tent. Some Samis still live in mountain huts or at the coastline during the summer months. They move down to the lowlands for the winter, constructing a tent called a *lavvo*. Samis make the simple lavvo from strong sticks, with which they build a frame. They cover the sticks with reindeer skins or, in recent years, canvas.

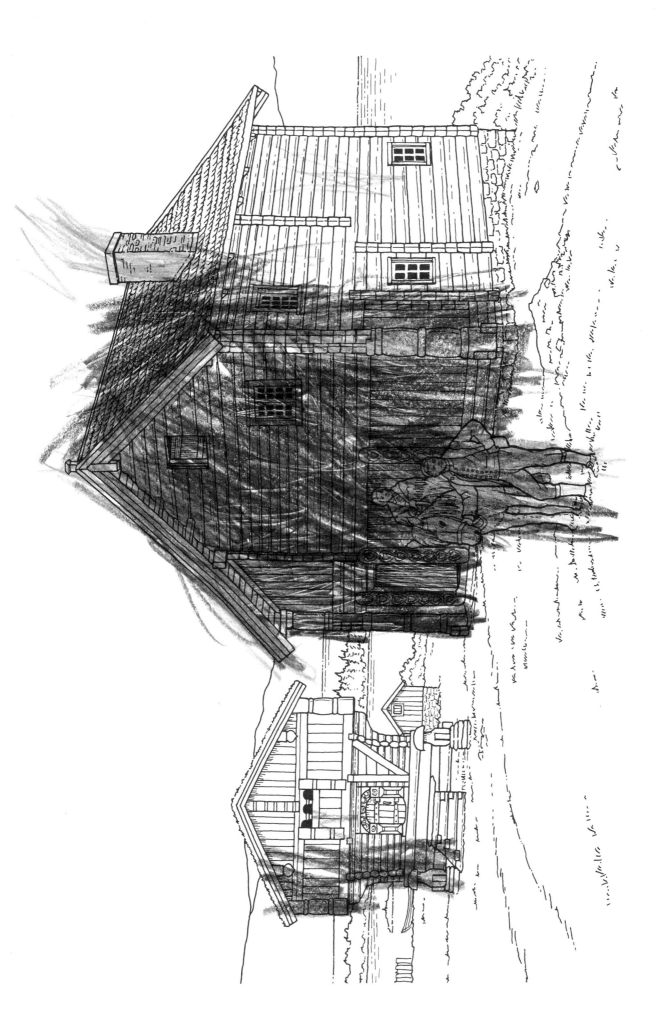

30. House and Loft, Norway (Europe). Farming in Norway has always been linked to two other great Norwegian industries—fishing and forestry. Traditional country homes in Norway consisted of a wood frame, glass windows, and a tile roof. Wood is the favorite construction material in this rugged land, which is heavily forested, especially with pine and birch. Careful construction helps these structures withstand the harsh winter weather.

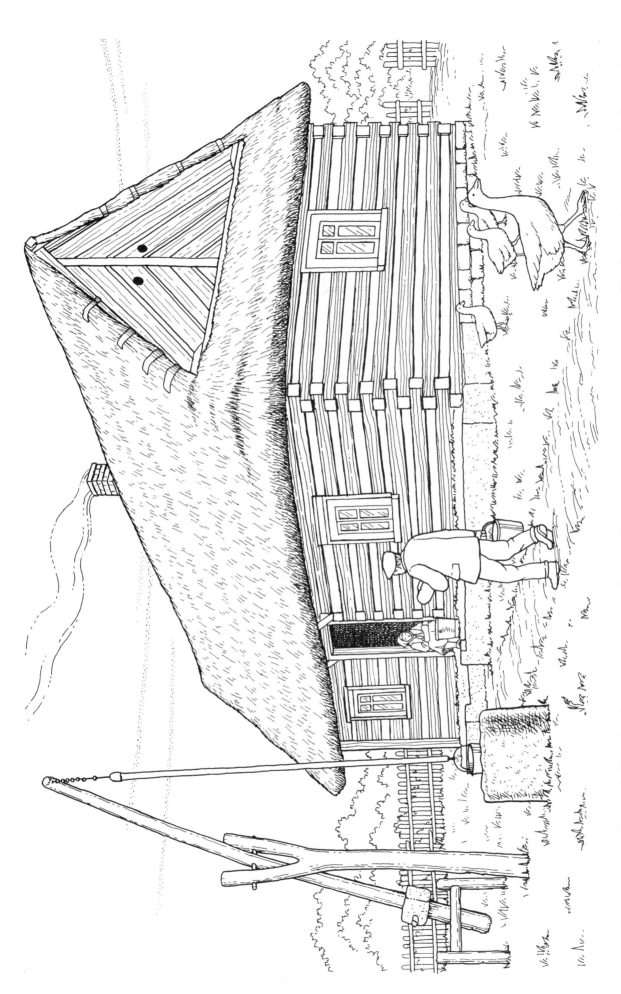

31. Farmhouse, Poland (Europe). This farmhouse is constructed somewhat like a pioneer log cabin. Split logs are arranged so that they fit together at the corners of the building in a crisscross pattern. This farmhouse features a thatched roof with an upper storage space; the roof slopes in order to shed summer rains and winter snow. The house shown here is built on a base in order to raise the wooden framework, providing storage space and protecting the wood from the damp ground.

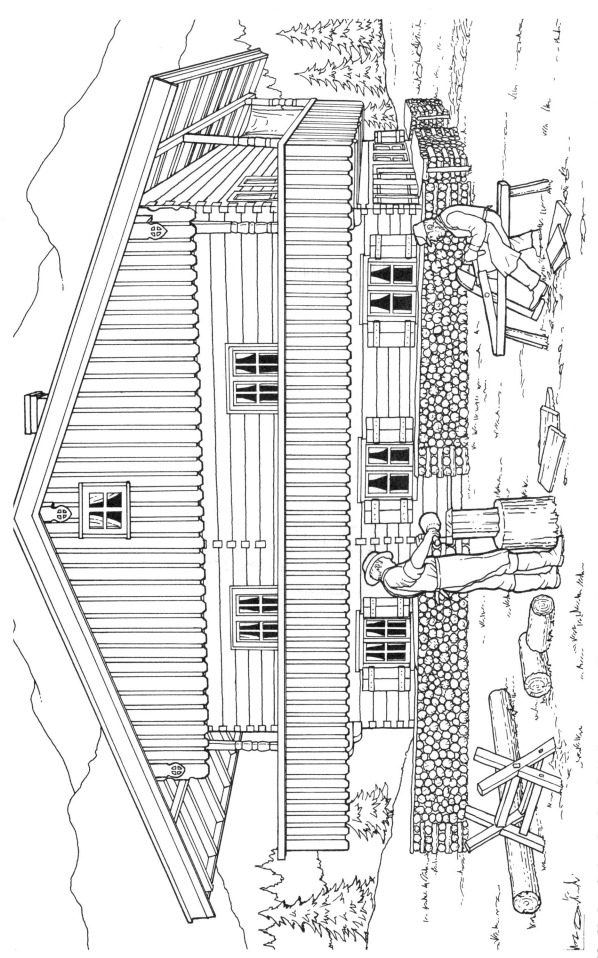

32. Chalet, Switzerland and Alpine regions (Europe). The typical Swiss chalet—an Alpine farmhouse found in the mountains and valleys of Switzerland, Austria, and southern Germany—traditionally consisted of two stories and an upper level capped by a sloping roof. A thick coating of snow helped keep in heat. Strict fire safety laws were put in place because of the use of wood in the chalet's construction. In some chalets, the ground floor was used as a stable during the snowy winter months.

33. Six-Timbered Haida Longhouse, Alaska and Queen Charlotte Islands (North America). The Haida, North American Indians, typically built a dwelling of six wooden beams and a pitched roof, supported by wooden beams. As shown above, the walls were made of vertical boards secured by horizontal timbers. This 19th-century style of building was one of two types found in Haida villages. An outstanding element of the Haida house was the towering totem pole, carved from red cedar, displaying representations of natural and supernatural animal figures.

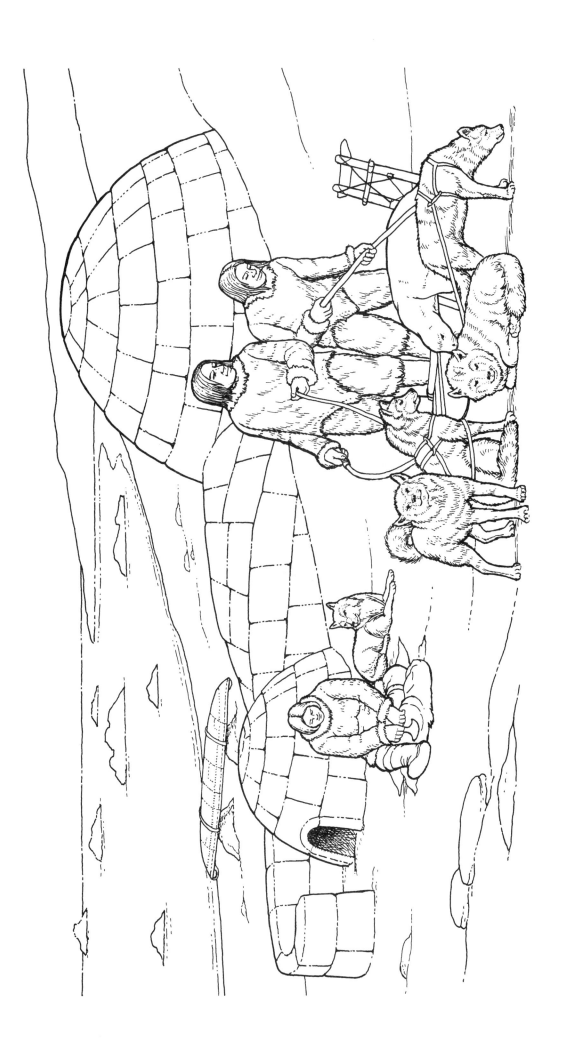

34. Inuit Igloo, Arctic region (North America). The Inuit of the Arctic region build houses with material easily available to them: snow. Building an igloo succeeds only if the right type of snow is used—it must be hard, not powdery. Blocks of snow are arranged, one on top of another. The Inuit builds inward and reduces the size of the blocks as he goes along. After completing the dome, he cuts out an opening and builds an entranceway. Skins covering the walls of the igloo help trap heat provided by a small fire.

35. Mesa Verde Cliff Houses, Colorado (North America). Brick buildings at Mesa Verde National Park in Colorado signal the presence of a North American Indian pueblo culture dating back to A.D. 1100–1300. The caves into which the cliff dwellings were built probably were inhabited as far back as 10,000 B.C. The dwellings shown here represent some of the hundreds found, many of which have been studied by archaeologists interested in the physical remains of early Native American communities.

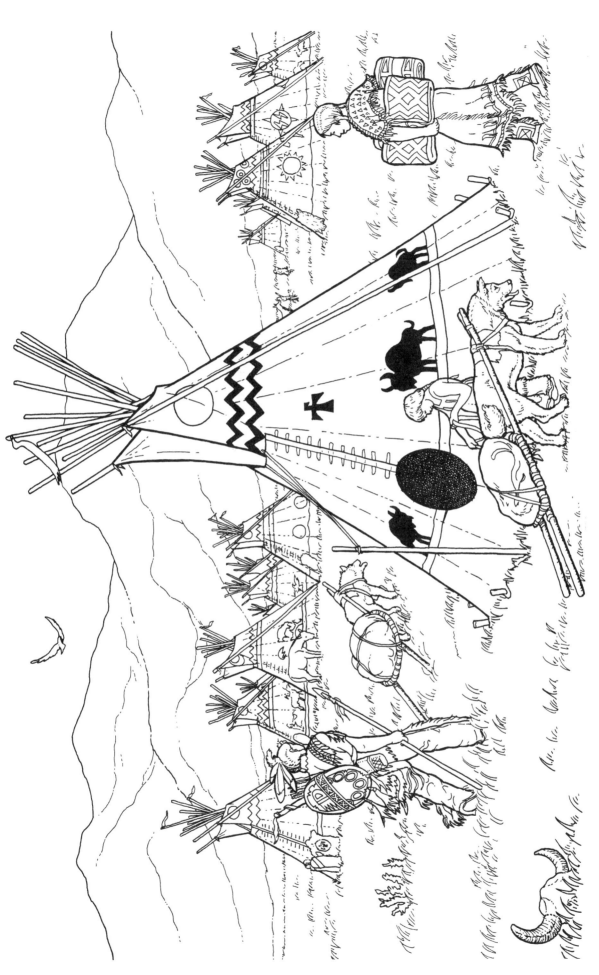

36. Plains Indian Tepee, Great Plains, U.S. (North America). The Plains Indians are known for their distinctive cone-shaped dwelling, the tepee. These Indians followed the buffalo herds, so they needed housing that could be set up and broken down quickly. A tepee was constructed by binding several long poles together and then standing them on the ground. More poles were set against the frame, and a covering of buffalo skin was stretched over the frame. The tepee had a flap at the top to let out smoke from the cooking fire. Plains Indian women set up and dismantled the tepees.

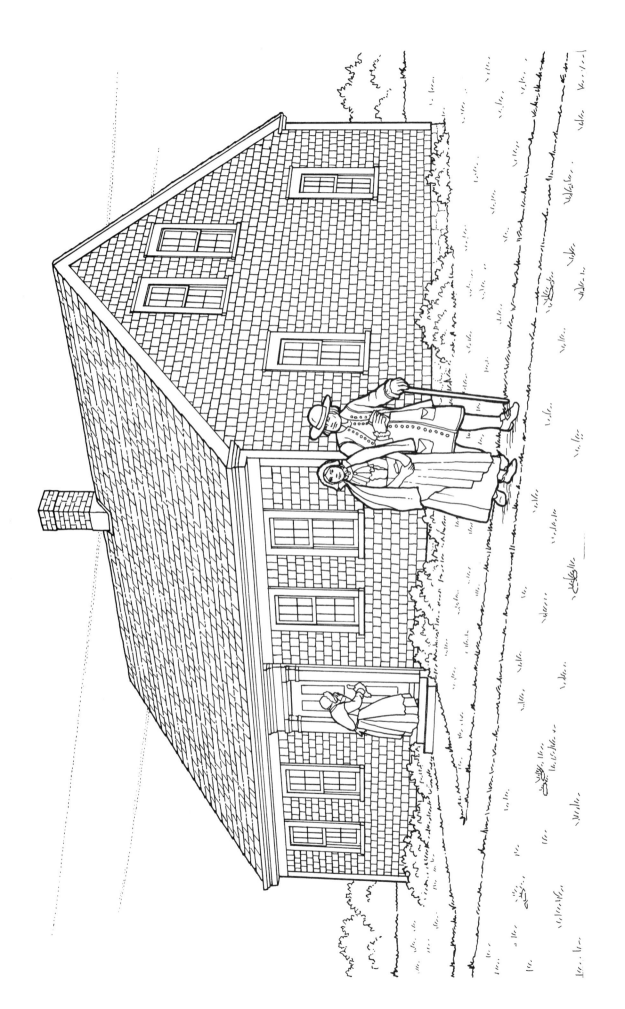

37. Cape Cod House, Massachusetts (North America). The settlers of this New England area built houses during the late 17th and early 18th centuries. Typically, they were solidly built brick buildings, rectangular and with sloping roofs, and displaying evenly spaced windows all around. A centrally located chimney vented heating and cooking fumes. Brick was a good material to use in the Cape Cod region, which was subject to wind and salt air due to its proximity to the water and its harsh winters.

38. Huichol Rancho, Mexico (North America). The Huichol rancho, or farm, is the dwelling place for North American Indians who live in the mountains in western Mexico. The dwelling is a hut that the Huichol Indians construct using mud bricks (adobe) and stone. They provide the rancho with a thatched roof to keep out the rain. Because of the harsh winters in this climate, the houses do not have windows, which might let in the bitterly cold mountain air.

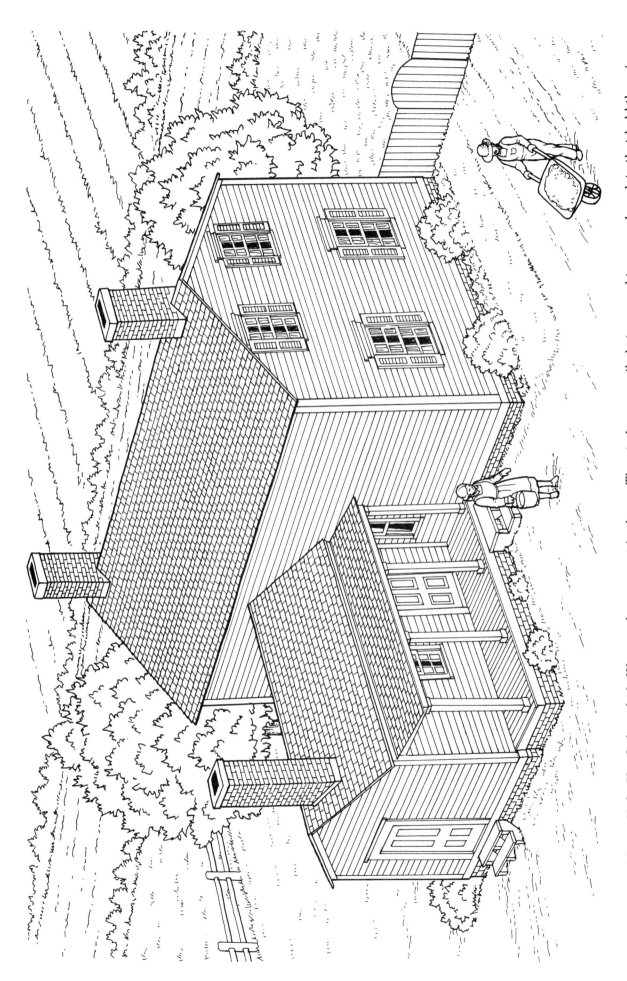

39. Farmhouse, Midwest U. S. (North America). Westward movement in the 19th century led to the need for permanent housing. One solution was the frame farmhouse. Rather than building cheaply, the farmer invested in skilled carpentry, using steel nails and uniformly cut wooden studs (vertical posts).

The studs were nailed at one end to a wooden plate that held them in a row. The studs were then nailed at the other end to a second plate. The roof was attached to this sturdy framework. Shuttered windows and a brick roof completed the farmhouse.

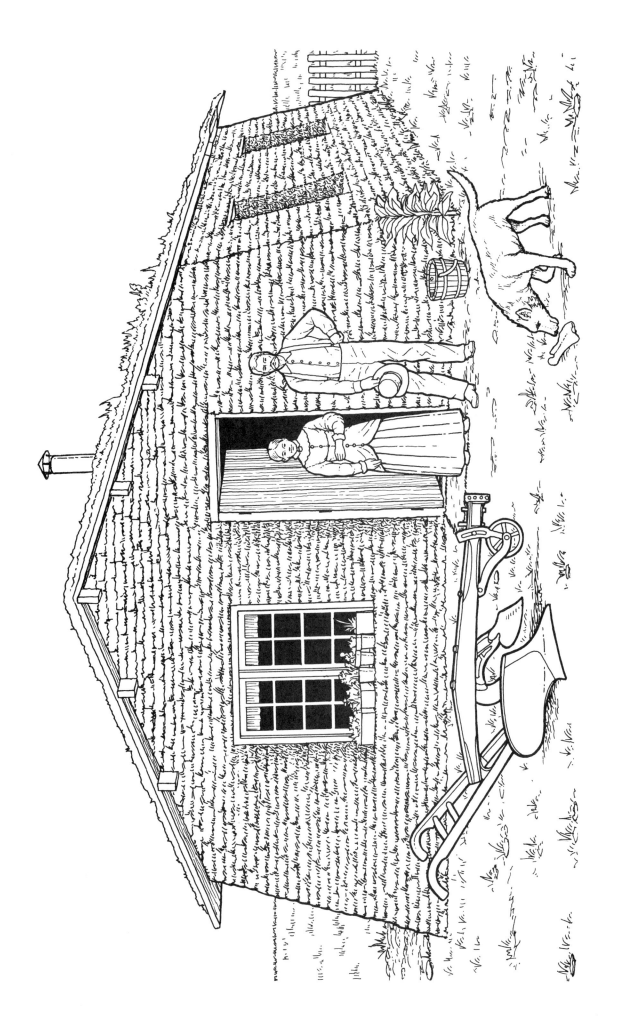

40. Sod House, Nebraska (North America). Many pioneer families settled in timbered areas that provided wood for house construction, but those who chose the vast grassy stretches of the west central region had to apply their resourcefulness to their environment. Nineteenth-century farmers on the treeless Nebraska plains used the native sod to build houses. They cut the sod into strips using special plows and then used the strips as bricks. Sod proved to be durable, protecting the settlers even during the harsh winter, and it acted as an insulator during winter and summer weather.

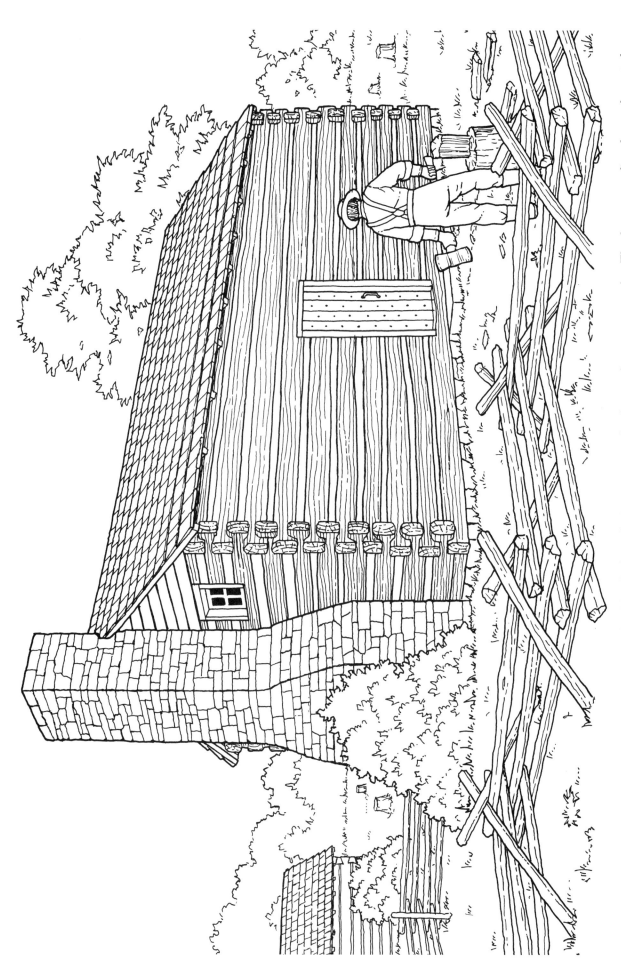

41. North American Frontier Log Cabin, Pennsylvania (North America). The pioneer log cabin, associated with the westward movement of American settlers, resembled the wooden structures in the northern European lands from which many pioneers came. In North America, the frontiersman constructed a house from tree trunks. The logs were fitted together at the corners of the house in an interlocking dovetail pattern for permanence. Wooden tiles—called shakes or shingles—were used to construct the roof atop the log supports. A stone chimney stood at one end of the cabin.

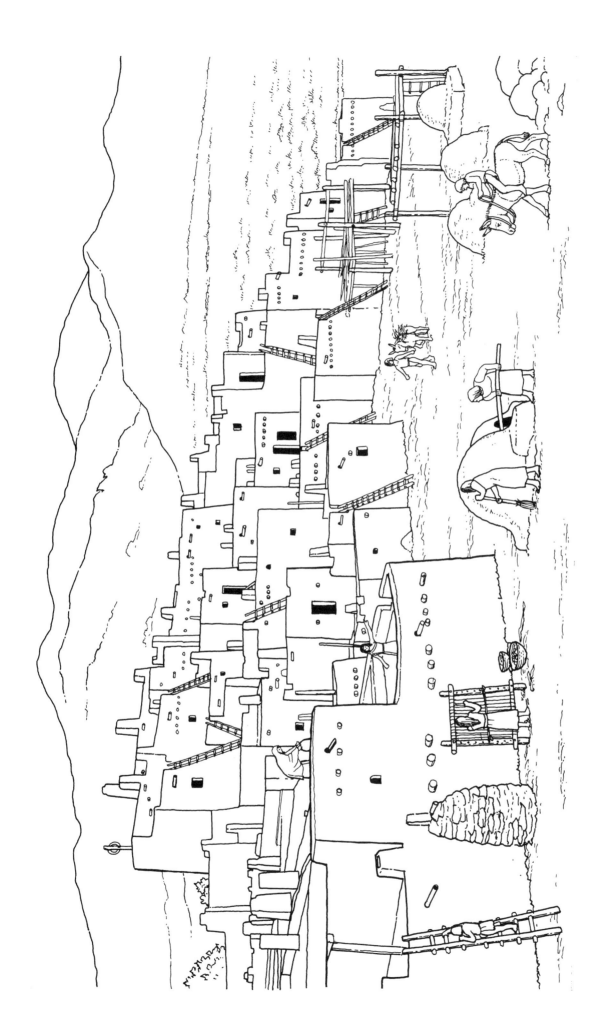

42. Pueblo, Southwest U. S. (North America). The Pueblo Indians lived in the present-day states of Arizona and New Mexico (*Pueblo* is the name given by Spanish settlers to both the peasant village and the people who lived there). The Pueblo built adobe (mud-brick) or stone structures several stories high. The houses, which sheltered one family in a single room, were built next to each other; as more houses were built, the floor of one house became the roof of another. Some pueblos were entered by climbing a ladder and going through a hole in the house's roof.

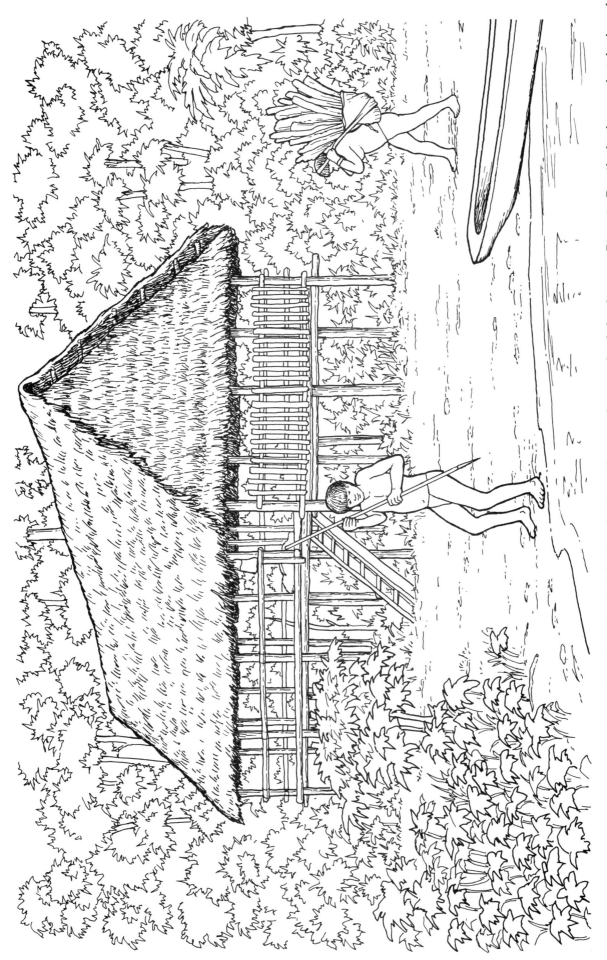

43. Amazon Delta Stilt House, Brazil (South America). Pacific Islanders built stilt houses over three thousand years ago, and this method has endured and spread to other regions as a means of adapting housing to a watery environment, as well as providing a safe haven in an area where floods are common. Here, at the mouth of the Amazon River in Brazil, the heavy thatched roof used by the region's Indians protects them from the rain and the sun, and the open framework allows for air circulation in this hot, humid climate.

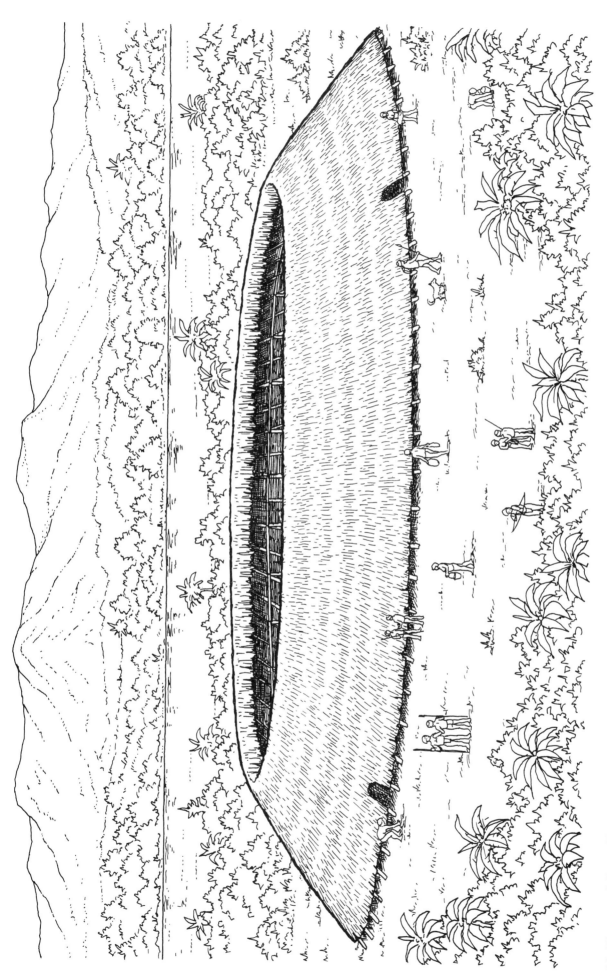

44. Yanomami Roundhouse, Brazil (South America). The Yanomami Indians live in an enormous structure called a roundhouse, an oval dwelling of woven palm leaves covering a support structure of poles. As shown above, the roundhouse is open at its center; therefore, the people living in it stay close to the outer wall. The communal living within the roundhouse is marked by a lack of interior walls. Each family has a fire for cooking. Family members sleep in hammocks around the fire. Poles are used both to suspend the hammocks and to mark off boundaries of each family's living space.

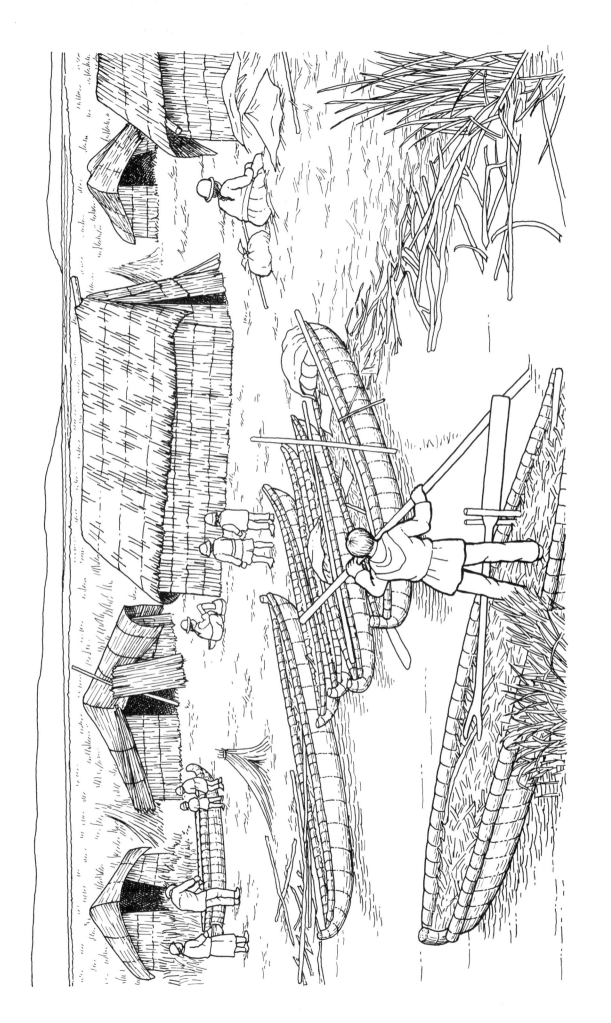

45. Lake Titicaca Reed Houses, Peru (South America). Reeds are very much a part of the lives of those who live near Lake Titicaca. Huts such as the ones shown here are a traditional form of housing for South American Indians of the region. Reeds are somewhat durable, but they must be replaced as they rot in this watery climate. Bedding is also made from reeds, as are the boats, also shown above. Here is an example of a plentiful local material that has traditionally been used to provide housing; its main drawback is that it is perishable and must continually be replaced.